The book of Psalms, paraphrased
for young readers.

This book belongs to:

Psalms are found in the Bible, in the Old Testament. They were written to express thoughts and emotions like praise, hope, joy, sadness, fear and many more. But people also write psalms today. Psalms are songs, poems or prayers.

These paraphrased Bible Psalms show us that talking to God is simple, like talking to a very close friend. It helps to talk about our thoughts and feelings as well as our dreams and wishes.

You can use can this book as a little "talking to God" starter, when you don't know what to say or how to put emotions into words. Even big people sometimes don't know what to say, and that's okay.

Little by little, you will get more comfortable with talking to God on your own, in a prayer or with a song, or maybe even writing your own little psalm.

How
to use this book?

1. Read a Psalm each day, before starting your day.

2. Read a Psalm together as a family during breakfast time, then say a prayer/Psalm in your own words.

3. Keep this book by your bed and read a Psalm before going to sleep at night.

4. Read a Psalm, then write down all the words that you remember from it. Take time to think about those specific words.

5. Pick out a favorite sentence from your Psalm for the day and write it down in your notebook.

6. Open the book and read a Psalm chosen at random.

7. Have someone pick a number from 1-150 for you, and then read them that Psalm.

8. Read a Psalm as your own prayer and reflect on it.

Always in Bloom

It makes me happy to do the right thing. I sit in a quiet place and I read your Word. I think about it during the day until I go to sleep. It makes me feel strong, like a tree planted near a stream of water. And then I'm always in bloom. I grow and bear fresh juicy fruit without drying up. God, you watch over me and all is well.

Be Wise

Why do some people get angry and make plans against you, God, and against the one you have chosen? Even at school, sometimes people talk bad or laugh about you. But one day, you'll have the last laugh and they will be sorry. Let's be wise and look to you, to do what's right. I will celebrate and honor you, because you provide for me. I won't ever regret putting my trust in you, God.

STAND STRONG

PSALM 3

I'm having a bad day. Everyone seems to be against me, and they make fun of me... But you, God, are like a strong shield. You give me courage to be strong inside. I send a prayer signal and your answer comes like a mighty mountain. I feel so much better to know that you are near.

GOOD NIGHT

I smile and beam with joy because you've helped me through the day. I list my highs and say thank you, God. I must be even happier than those who are rich. I have all I need to be fully content. Now I can go to bed and sleep in peace because you take care of everything and keep me safe.

PSALM 4

PSALM 5

Good morning, God! I need your help for today, well, actually for every day. Thank you for inviting me to spend this time with you. Every morning I come and tip-toe close to you and I wait for your directions, because you know how to keep me from getting in trouble. I know you aren't pleased with those who disobey and tell lies, or those who hurt or trick others. But you welcome me with open arms. It makes me happy to do what is right.

GOOD MORNING

A PUDDLE OF TEARS

I don't want any more yelling.
I don't want more time-outs. I have a
tummy ache in my heart. My feelings got
hurt and I'm going to burst out and cry.
Now I'm in a puddle of tears. I know it's
okay to cry, but I want to feel better. I want
this to pass. God, I can talk to you about
anything because I know
you listen.

PSALM 6

GOD IS FAIR

Why did my hands hit that? Why did I get upset with a friend? Why did I mess up again? Why did I forget what Dad and Mom told me? Uh, oh! So many "why's"! Should I be punished? I don't have all the answers but I do know one thing; that you, God, are loving and fair. Whatever you do, you do it with love. Help me to learn my lesson and to do better next time.

PSALM 7

You're Awesome

PSALM 8

God, I shout your name, and it echoes your glory over every beautiful thing. Your name is like music to my ears. Since I was a baby I sang songs about you. I look up at the sky and I'm in awe. From the moon and the stars, all the way to the bottom of the ocean; everything shows thanks for your greatness. I feel so small, yet you still pay attention to little me. I can help take care of our pet, feed the little birds outside my window and water the garden. You give us this world to look after, and you're the one who makes it all beautiful.

I'm thanking you, God, from a full heart. I'm writing and drawing about your wonders. When things get messed up, you take over and set things right again. When I'm with you, I can shout victory because you have power over everything. So I whistle, I laugh, and I jump for joy.

V

V FOR VICTORY

God, sometimes we complain about what we don't like. "It should be done THIS way!" we say. Or "Why did this happen to me?" We play the blame game and find someone else to accuse for our problems. God, sometimes we even blame you. But problems and difficulties are occasions for you to do something. Ugliness is a chance to make beautiful. Sadness is a chance to make glad. God, you are always available to us. I know that you'll make things right. In you is goodness.

ONLY GOOD

PSALM 10

SETTING THINGS RIGHT

Hey, little birdie friend. Don't worry, I'll keep you safe. When I'm scared, I run for cover too. I run to God. I can always find him because his address never changes. I know where he is. I just close my eyes and sit real quiet and he's there. God, you always keep your eyes on me, without even blinking. You're the boss of setting things right. You make crooked lines straight. You make me stand up after I fall down. I know I can count on you for help. Not just 1 time, or 2, 3 or 4, but many, many times more.

PSALM 11

How could he? My friend said something about me that wasn't true. Now I can't even face the other kids anymore. They'll think bad about me. Ouchy! Lies really hurt and leave an ouchy in my heart. What am I going to do now? God, your mouth never tells a lie. Please help me not to lie. Help me to always say things that are true. Now I see how much it hurts when someone lies.

No LIES

LONG ENOUGH

I was sick with a tummy ache and I couldn't go over to my friend's house to play. I had to stay in bed and get extra rest. Then I had to wait before seeing him in case it was contagious. That meant I had to wait a long time. Hours and hours and hours long. But since I'm all better now, I think it's long enough. God, what do you think? Thank you, God. I'm so glad you took away this tummy ache. Now I need to go visit my friend to get rid of this lonely ache.

How Many?

God, you're poking your head out from heaven to say peekaboo! You're looking at all the people, to find a wise person, who looks to you for help and who wants to please you. How many are there? Zero? None at all? It seems that bad people are everywhere. But God, I pray that good people will take action, so we can be glad. You are with those who do what is right.

PSALM 14

YOU'RE INVITED!

A SLEEP-OVER PARTY

God, who gets invited to a sleep-over party at your place? Can I be on the guest list? Oh wait, don't tell me, I know. You welcome those who are loving and kind. Who show respect and tell the truth. Those who don't hurt their friends or blame their neighbors. Those who keep their promises and who don't get into trouble when Dad and Mom are not looking. Hey, come to think of it, I'd invite those friends to my party too, any day.

Inside and Out

God, every beautiful flower and amazing creature comes from you. I have great friends because of you too. But I pick you as my very bestest friend forever. Not just like a brand name or something. God, you're a million times bigger, and your love is a million times stronger than anything that has ever existed. People can only hug and kiss and love from the outside, but you, God, can love us on the inside. You know things and people from the inside too, though we only know them from the outside. I have so much more to learn about you.

PSALM 16

LOTS TO SAY

God, I have so much to tell you. So many words need to come out. I know you already know everything because you can see right inside of me. But you don't mind me blabbing to you, right? Talking to you makes me feel so much better. Sometimes I feel like running and hiding away because I don't want to get hurt. Other times life is too loud and noisy and problems get so messy. Can you hide me under your wings and keep me safe forever?

PSALM 17

A STRONG SHIELD

I love you, God. You tower way up high. You are like my strong castle, my rescuing knight. I hide behind your shield and I feel completely safe. I sing songs to show you my thanks. I experience your strength and your goodness each day. Happy family times, love and care, good food, play times, safe times. All that you do gives me such a bounce.

PSALM 19

God, your glory shines like fireworks in the sky. The day and the night tell the amazing story of what you can do. The sun gives heat from the time it rises all the way till it sets. Your Word comforts and cuddles and warms up my heart. Each word teaches me something new. It makes simple people like me think about wise things. All you say is good and true. I bet your words are better than all the money in the world. And they're even sweeter than the juiciest berries or carrot cake. They're like my guide map, showing me where to go.

SKY CRAFTS

GOD ANSWERS

PSALM 20

Yay! God, you answered my prayer. I passed the test and I won the relay race game! I'll dance a parade and raise the roof up with joy. My wins are in thanks to you. You helped me study real hard and you gave me strength to keep going even when I felt like stopping. Now I'm making you a flower bouquet. I'm setting up balloons and garlands all over. I celebrate this happy day with you!

Piles of Blessings

I'm blessed like a king. God, you load me with gifts and your arms welcome me with love. Every day, this pile of blessings grows. I have clothes of every color of the rainbow, I have a cozy bed and a bright window facing the birds in the trees. I have stripped curtains and a zoo of stuffed animals. If I could, I'd smile from my head to my toes. God, no one at all should miss out on this. Let me tell everyone of your goodness.

PSALM 21

WHAT A MESS

Oh, God, why are things going wrong? I feel like everything is tumbling over and I'm in a big fat mess. Why do my friends seem to have it so good? They seem to get to do what they want; they don't have to clean up... God, does no one care about me? I just feel like a tiny ant on the floor. And when I made a mistake and kicked over the pot, dirt spilled out all over and everyone poked fun at me and made faces. God, hurry up and help me, please. I know you can. And when you do, I'll shout it out. I'll tell all my friends that you care and that you love, even when I messed up.

My Shepherd

Dear God, you are like my shepherd. With you, I don't need a thing. You think of it all. You prepare a place for me to rest; the soft green grass tickles my nose. You give me a fresh drink of water. As you promise, you point the way for me to go. If the path gets dark, I'm not afraid, when you walk by my side. Your trusty shepherd's stick makes me feel secure. You serve me a delicious meal; I am content. You lift my droopy head and I overflow with blessings. Your goodness and love follow me every day of my life, until I arrive, safe at home with you, where I can stay forever and ever and even longer.

I'M HIS, HE'S MINE

The earth and everything in it belong to you, God. That includes me. You built it all, the oceans and rivers, the hills and the mountains. But who can reach up to you God, on your high mountain? Those who do what's right, those with an honest and kind heart. God, you are at my side and with your help I can make it. I'm waking up to a new day and I'm ready for the climb.

God, take me by the hand and lead me to the path of good things. The road that leads to you. That's why I make sure to follow the signs and read the directions. I keep my eyes fixed on you. Please don't let me get lost or break down. God, please watch over me and keep me out of trouble.

HE LEADS

PSALM 26

God, my eyes never
stop seeing your love. It's
everywhere I look. I want
to keep in step with you,
never missing
a beat.

NEVER
MISSED

God, I love living
with you. Your house
sparkles with love
and beauty.

LIGHT IN SIGHT

Brightness, light, spice, that's you, God! With you on my side I'm not afraid. When those big bullies come toward me, you help me stay calm and keep cool. Thank you. I ask you for one thing, God. Please can I come and live in your house? It's beautiful and quiet, safe from noisy bad bullies and free from monster trouble. When my day feels like a traffic jam, your home feels like the perfect vacation spot. Light up the path that leads to you so I can come at any time I need some peace. And I will sing and dance for joy. I will be patient through the bad days. I will be strong.

PSALM 27

BOUNCE FOR JOY

I call to you, God. I lift up my arms as I call for help. And you come to the rescue. You make my heart feel better again. Now I know that you're on my side. I bounce for joy and shout hooray as I sing my thanks. You are strength to every bunny. You care for us like a good shepherd.

GIANT STRENGTH

Bravo, God, bravo! Encore, encore! I'm in awe at this glorious show of power. I put on my very best clothes for this special event. Across the sky, flashing lights and thunderbolts tell of your greatness. Across the seas, power-waves and waters speak of your strength. The trees dance, the deserts shake, the mountains jump for joy and the leaves fall. They all shout "Glory to God!". You control the world. You give your people strength and bring us peace.

PSALM 29

Thank you, God. I wasn't too careful and I made things fall apart, but you gave me another chance. Sometimes I make a mess of things. I'm clumsy or too bouncy. It makes others a bit angry at times. But across my whole lifetime there is so much love. My feelings are hurt and I cry tears that run down to my toes, but then later on I can laugh again. You have turned my sadness into dancing. I want to sing your love at the top of my voice.

GOD'S FAVOR

Not Afraid

God, I run to you for help. Please come down here so you can hear me. You're my cave to hide in, my shelter from storms of trouble, my road back to safety. I'm dancing in circles of your love. Problems make me tired. There are neighbors that make fun of me. There are friends that ignore me, and others that say bad things about me. Save me from this unkind world. Help me to be strong and not give up. I know you'll help me get through this.

PSALM 31

HONEST HEARTS

PSALM 32

I couldn't talk about it. I was embarrassed. But the longer it stayed inside, the yuckier I felt. I didn't want to say anything because I was afraid of getting into trouble. What would others think of me? But finally, I was honest about my wrongdoing, and it came out like a big volcano burst! Boom! Wow! Now I feel relief and peace. First I talked with you in prayer, then I told my parents. We had a good discussion time. I apologized, I forgave, I felt better. Honest hearts need a celebration! Shout hurray!

Good people cheer for you, God. Honest people praise you. I'm having a musical flower party to celebrate. Everything you say is true and right. You blew the stars into place. You poured water to make the seas. All creatures sit in respect and say thank you. My heart bursts with joy because your love pours out all over me.

OH, JOY!

PSALM 33

GOD'S GOODNESS

At any chance I get, I say thank you, God. My lungs and heart fill up with praise. From my head to my tummy; from my tummy to my toes, I show thanks. I invite all my friends to join me! Now let's give our biggest smiles to God, so he can take our photo and remember us. Then I open my mouth and taste your goodness. It's yummy! I open my eyes and see your goodness. It's pretty! Thank you, God, for giving me the very best. I don't lack anything. Being this happy makes me think of throwing out love confetti. And I feel like I could bubble out kindness to overflowing.

PSALM 34

SAVE ME!

God, stand up for me, please. Bullies and spiders, flies and robbers, they bother me. I want to bounce freely, celebrating life, without fear. Save me, please! No one can help me like you do. Every bone in my body wants to laugh and sing about how good you are. Oh no, but here comes a mosquito. Please get it away from me! Now my friends and I can shout again and again, that you are great! You take care of everything.

God, I'm here to fill up on love. Your love is everywhere. It reaches above the clouds and your faithfulness goes farther than crowds. Your goodness reaches past the tallest mountain and you are far and wide as the biggest ocean. But no matter how big you are, you still care about the smallest creature like me. Thank you, God, for tasty picnic treats and fresh drinks of pleasure. You light up my path and each step is a bounce of joy.

PSALM 36

Filled Up

In on the Best

I don't bother trying to be like someone else, I just try to be the best me that I can be. I wouldn't make a very good carrot, so I just continue being the bunny that enjoys digging them up. Others may have more than me or better things than me. But because I matter to you, you let me in on the best, just what I need. God, what I care about most, is keeping company with you.

God, I'm stuck in this sick bed, under this heavy blanket. My mouth is shut with this thermometer and my nose is all stuffed up with a cold. My eyes are teary and my heart is empty. My friends and cousins can't even visit. I'm so bored and lonely. Well, all I can do is wait. I'm waiting as you heal my body. But please don't forget about me. I'm looking forward to being well again.

When I'm sick

PSALM 38

I'M HERE HOPING

Hey, little feet, be careful where you go.
Hey, little tongue, be careful what you say.
God, I'm hoping and wishing "upon a flower", that you will hear my prayer today. I don't want to take a wrong step. I don't want bad words to come out of my mouth. Sometimes I just need to be still and wait a while, until I feel ready to get on with my day.

PSALM 40

I waited and waited and waited for you, God. At last, you heard my cry and you came to the rescue. You picked me up from the ditch and you pulled me out of the muddy puddle. You put me in a safe place, so that I wouldn't slip and fall again. And you taught me a song. Now I sing my song everyday. Those who hear it are glad. "God, I can trust you, I know I can. No one compares to you, not even 1 or 2. I try to say it in words or count it in numbers, but you're just too grand." You don't expect me to sing perfectly. You let me be myself. And so I sing with the best voice I have, and with all the love my heart can hold.

I WAITED PATIENTLY

Put me back together

Sometimes I feel so small and weak. I can't do important things. But God, you look after me and I'm growing strong. I'm lucky to be in such good care. When I'm sick, you come and nurse me back to health. You put all the broken pieces back together. When I'm back on my feet, I'll bounce for joy and shout victory. I'll tell everyone that you are great for always and always and always.

PSALM 41

I'M THIRSTY

Animals drink from the creek, people drink from the tap. Sometimes I feel like I need a drink from you, God. I'm thirsty for you. I don't make it for very long without spending some time with you. When I'm on a bummer and I cry for no reason, I know that it's time to fill up on a drink of you. And soon I'm joyful again. You make me smile. The next time I feel grumpy, let me remember this. And come and splash your joy all over me again.

MY GUIDE

God, I need a flashlight when life gets foggy and dark. Please show me your map so I can find my way to you. I love to spend time with you, up on your mountaintop. It's so quiet and peaceful. And the view is incredible! I play my musical instrument and I sing songs about you. There are no cares, no worries or sadness when I'm up here with you. I look to you, my God of wonder.

Since a teeny tiny bunny, I read stories and stories about you, God. How you led your people to a safe place, how you gave them a place to live. How you got them out of trouble. You smiled as you gave them pocketfuls of gifts and blessings. But can you still help little ones like me today? If so, please don't leave me stuck here. Quickly, quickly, God, send someone to help me! I don't want to end up flat on my face in the dirt, again. I need a little hand here, or maybe a big giant heap of help.

I'M COUNTING ON YOU

YOU ARE MY KING

Today, these words bubble in my heart, as I write this letter to you, my king: You are the most honorable, and the wisest of all. God has blessed you forever. Confident and courageous, you ride on to victory. You take defense for the truth, for kindness and for justice. Because God has chosen you as king, you will take action for what's right. May you reign forever and ever. And, just so you know, I'm your biggest fan. Love Bunny

MY HIDING PLACE

God, you are a safe place to hide. You are always there when I need you. I don't have to be afraid of an earthquake or a rush of waves, or moving mountains. You are like an army that protects. Fountains splash joy, keeping me cool. That's your home, where the streets are safe and where you and I can hang out together in a quiet place. You make it all beautiful, with flowers and trees and butterflies. You stop wars and you break up weapons. That's it, God! Show your strong power!

PSALM 46

JOY

A SHOUT FOR JOY

Clap hands, everyone! Shout it out with your loudest voice, "God is wonderful!" You're my king. I cheer for you, God! I bounce up, higher and higher, and burst with joy. You sit on your holy throne and I sing you my very best song. I hope you like it. Now the trumpets sound. Toot! Toot! And the drum rolls. Ba-dum-chhh! You are the God of the whole earth. Everyone brings you their praise and respect.

GOD'S CITY

God, you are great, you should be praised. Your city is high and beautiful. It brings joy to the whole world. You are there and you keep it safe. When I come for a visit, I see your love in action. Your arms are heaped with goodness. And when I say your name, a long train of thanks follows behind. I'm so happy; I feel I could dance. This is a story I'm going to tell my kids and grandkids about. The story of you! How you live and guide and protect, for always.

PSALM 48

Sometimes people brag about their stuff, and sometimes I wish I had more money to buy more stuff. But money can't buy everything, at least not the really important things. It can't buy joy and a family that loves me. It can't buy a good friend either. Rich people trust in their money, but they can't take money or all their fancy stuff with them when they die. Money doesn't make them live forever. So I don't need to compare with the rich and the famous. Stuff and money pass away and get old and used up. I am glad to be alive and I trust God and live with honesty.

MONEY AND STUFF

OUR MEETING PLACE

God, you are calling all of creation to get together. You make a grand entrance, with fireworks and sparkling lights. You call my name. "Here I am!" I say. Then I sit still and listen. I'm proud to be invited, and most of all, to know that I belong to you. I will prepare a banquet of praise and a feast of loving deeds to you. I will never forget you, God.

I NEED A SCRUB

Dear God. I've done some messy actions. Please wash away my bad marks and clean my icky feelings. And my heart needs a spring cleaning because I've been naughty. I am ready to do what is fair and right. My actions can get kind of smelly at times, and I need a good soak with lots of soap. And after a good scrub I can start again and be sparkling clean like fresh snow. I will do better this time, because I have learned more. Thank you for giving me another chance. I dance and sing, because you make me feel brand new.

Bullies brag about the bad things they do. But what good does it bring to say hurtful words? Doesn't it turn to wilt, when they lie and cheat? I'd rather be like a tree that grows big and green, that gives loving shade and shelter to friends and those around. I trust in God, because he is good and his love is forever and ever.

TREES OF EASE

ASK FOR HELP

PSALM 53

God, you are looking for those who are wise, those who are humble to ask for help. But some choose to go their own way and do their own thing. They don't want to listen to good advice. But I'm not too proud to ask for help. Especially since you know how thing works best. I come to you when I need help because you can take things upside down and turn them right side up again.

PSALM 54

Dear God, please hear my prayer today. Please listen. I feel so alone. Sometimes I have the impression that nobody loves me. No one is choosing me to be on their team. They don't think I'm good enough cause I seem so small and weak. Please take my side. Be on my team so they can see that you are strong. I want to run fast like the wind. Thank you, God, that you stick close beside me. Together, we are the perfect team.

I NEED HELP

Good friends are kind and gentle. They don't shout and argue. They talk things out. Fake friends only want the best you have and then turn against you. God, you are the bestest friend. You don't run off when I have an ache. You don't leave me when snack is all done. You don't throw a fit when we don't play your game. I want to be the bestest friend too. I want to work things out peacefully, to have fun and get along with others.

TRUE FRIENDS

HIGHS AND LOWS

PSALM 56

God, let me tell you about my day. Well, I did have some lows. Sluggy ate my salad and Bunny stepped on my toes. Spiderman bit my nose. I feel upset about all that. But I trust you God. There are also a lot of highs to my day: Even though my bed was a little hard, my pillow was nice and soft. Mom took me shopping as she promised, and I found a nice brush for my whiskers. I rode my bike to school today, and I didn't fall over. Dad made my favorite carrot cake for dinner. God, thank you for being there, in the good things and the bad.

Hi God! I'm taking a ride. Can you see me up here? I know I can count on you because you hold this whole world together. From up here I see all its beauty. I thank you and sing songs out loud! Can everyone down there hear me? Everyone should know about your love. Your love keeps me going higher and higher. God, you are full of sparkling glory.

PSALM 57

GLORY IN THE HIGHEST

JUDGE WISELY

You're a wise judge, God. You do everything perfectly. Those who don't listen and pay attention, or who lie and cheat, make this game no fun at all. We must play by the rules and follow your instructions. Those who don't want to play fairly can leave the game. Kindness, respect and honesty are what makes games really fun. This game needs more of these kinds of players. You judge fairly and bless those who obey.

YOUR BIG LOVE

PSALM 59

My strong God, I can always count on you. Your love always shows up right on time when I need help. I know that you rule well, everywhere that you're in charge. It's so sad to see those naughty bullies who hurt and play mean tricks. It makes me sad I feel bothered by them. But you can handle the situation. You just point your finger or think it, and it's done. You take care of it in fine style. And I sing your greatness. I sing because you are strong. Your great love keeps me safe and stands up for me, each time.

Oh, God, there you are! I need help! I set out all happy this morning, but... things just tumbled about me and each task became bigger and bigger. I ate my favorite breakfast, but then I had homework to do. That took away my cheer. Mom called me to make my bed. That took away my smile. Later, Dad asked me to help in the garden. That took away my bounce. It all seems too much for me! My hands are almost ouchy now. God, please help me with the difficult things. You are big and strong enough for the both of us.

IT'S TOO MUCH

PSALM 61

PROTECT ME

I take a walk up the hill to the end of the garden. It's so quiet here, a perfect place to get away. I sit on a low branch. Oh, so this is where the birds hang out. God, you protect me like a mama bird protects her babies. Please cover me with your wings so I can be safe from harm. I don't have to be afraid when I'm close to you. And you welcome me into your presence. I accept the invitation. I could hang out here every day, you know. And it's the perfect time to sing a song about your love and goodness. Goodness rhymes with sweetness, which rhymes with loveliness, and that all brings me fullness.

God, you're my very favorite. I'll wait here for you because everything I need comes from you. Why wouldn't it? You're a solid rock under my feet and breathing space for my soul. You're like a strong castle. I'm safe for life. God, you're my favorite. I'll wait here for you because everything I hope for comes from you. And why wouldn't it? Me and my friend and the whole world put together, are still not strong enough. But you, you're rock solid, iron strong. Imagine that!

SOLID ROCK

PSALM 63

HANG ON TO ME

It's been a hot day.
I feel so hungry and thirsty.
Can I have a taste of your
God-food. It's the best! I can't get enough of it.
It's even better than pizza and better than ice-cream. It doesn't just satisfy for a little while. God, I'm drinking of your strength and eating of your delicious love. I lick my lips clean. Now I'm feeling fully satisfied. I stretch out my arms like banners of praise to you. When I get sleepy, I close my eyes and dream about your goodness. And then I have all the energy again to run and play. I even take a swing, as I hold on tight to you. But I don't have to worry, cause you also hold on to me. You never let go of me. I'm safe.

When i'm afraid

God, I've got a problem. There are meanies that are out to get me. Keep me safe as I hide here. Don't let them find me. They say mean things that hurt innocent people. They encourage each other to do wrong. They talk about setting traps. They think they're so clever and that no one will stop them. But, God, you see the wrong. Don't let them get away with it. Open their eyes to want to change. Take the side of those who do what's right and who make peace. We will speak up and rejoice and thank you, because you keep us safe.

PSALM 64

God, the whole earth dances in your goodness. You bring spring showers to water the fields and to fill the streams. You paint the wheat fields golden and the flower petals all different colors. You make everything grow. The trees and plants blossom and bear fruit. Even sheep and cattle come to graze on the dancing hills. Let us sing and shout together because we are blessed. We are content and party in earth's fullness.

YOU MAKE IT GROW!

SING AND SHOUT

PSALM 66

All together now, let's clap for God. Nothing compares to you. The earth kneels to worship and bounces to sing. I take a look at your creation and it takes my breath away. That means I don't even know what to say because I'm in awe. Thank you, God! The shapes and colors and beauty all around make me want to celebrate and play. Look how the wind makes my kite dance in praise. Who wants to join us?

I SAY THANKS

God, I say grace and I thank you for this food. Yum! Yum! I enjoy it to the full. It comes from you, God. The earth is full of your gifts of goodness and it makes my tummy feel good too. Please bless it to my body, so I can grow strong and wise and continue to enjoy all that's good for me. Everyone should show off their thanks. This food is a blessing from you, God. From the tip of my tongue all the way to my tummy, I thank you.

PSALM 68

God, when I see you in action I laugh and I sing for joy. Yes, even in the rain. You just say the words and it happens. Sometimes it pours out in bucketfulls to help water the thirsty ground. A dry piece of land becomes an oasis. Other times just a few sprinkles give a little birdie a drink. You take charge over the land and over the mountains and give them just what they need. And God, let me be a fountain of praise to you. Bravo! Bravo! You bring power, thunder and beauty for us to enjoy.

YOU SEND THE RAIN

TO THE RESCUE

God, please come to my rescue and save me.
I tripped and slipped in the mud. Don't let me
get stuck in here. Ouchy! I got a scrape too.
When I'm in trouble I know that I can call your
name and you answer because you're full of love.
Everyone should know that they can call on you
too. You listen and you come quickly. You put
a cream on my scratch and a band aid on my
hurting heart. When I can't help myself, you
come to pick me up. I'm always safe with you.

God, please hurry! Come quickly, and help me!
I feel like the bullies are out to get me. They're
teasing me again. Take my defense, please. I will
not take revenge because it's for you alone to judge
them. If it were me, I'd teach them a good lesson.
They should feel embarrassed at their own jokes and
get hurt because of their own hurtful words. But you
take care of them as you see fit. And those who look
to you, let them be glad. Let them sing. Let them
say over and over again "God, you are awesome!
You're magnificent, you're grand!"

PSALM 70

COME QUICKLY

Young and Old

PSALM 71

God, continue to do what you do so well. You get me up on my feet when I'm weak. You're like a guest room when I need a quiet break. Your door is always open. Each morning you turn on the light of a new day. I wake up and I turn on my mouth to praise you. When I was a little baby you comforted me. When I was young, you taught me. But don't ever leave my side, not even when I get old and grey. As I write my journal of all the things you do for me, I never run out of things to say. I add in soooo many "thank you's" and "I love you's".

God, the best gift you could give a king is wisdom. The best gift for a prince is to rule well. Be a gift to the poor, as you stand up for the weak. A gift to the needy children; give them what they need. Be rain for the plants that burst into pretty blossoms on the earth. We want your gift of peace. Peace on earth so everything can be even more beautiful. You draw circles of blessings around me. Let me load you up with my humble gift too. Here it is. I lift up my praise and thank-you gift to you.

BEST GIFTS

PSALM 72

What Am I Looking At?

No doubt about it, God, you are good. Good to those who do what's right, good to those who are kind. Help me not to miss your goodness. But sometimes I don't see it because I'm too busy looking at others instead. They seem to have it better than me. I look at all their cool toys, their special shoes and fancy foods. It makes me feel bad because they're not always nice about it. They are proud and selfish. But why do I take my eyes off of what I have? It makes me forget that you have already blessed me with what I need. I don't ever have to worry that I don't have enough.

I NEED A SIGN

God, sometimes it seems like there is not a sign of you anywhere on this earth. I see so much hate. There are wars and very poor people who need help. Where are you when all this happens? Are you gone on vacation? Did you forgot about us? But I know you are God forever. You own the day and the night. You put the stars and the sun in place. The earth is yours, from top to bottom. You shape and color up the seasons; spring, summer, autumn and winter. Each one is a taste of wonder. I know I can trust you.

PSALM 74

MOST MYSTERIOUS

Can you guess, what is for me the most mysterious word? A word that is beyond us all... Yes, GOD. Your name is the biggest, the most awesome, the most fantastic! And when I practice my spelling, your name is also the easiest for me to remember. G.O.D. Your name spells God but it also spells goodness, love and victory. You have always been and you never end. You are a mystery and a wonder and I learn something new about you each day. It's nothing for you to take power away from the wicked, and give it to those who do good. God, good can always win because YOU always win!

PSALM 76

God, you are well known in town and around our neighborhood. And at home, we talk about you often. You're always there when we get up and when we go to sleep, and all the in-betweens. Brother, Sister and I made you special gifts. We give you our very best presents because you're the best! We set up balloons and ribbons too because we're having a party in your honor.
Hooray for God!

CALM ME

Dear God, I can't sleep. Can I talk to you? I'm laying here, wide awake. But why can't I sleep? Is something bothering me? Am I too excited? I don't know how to put my thoughts into words. So I just close my eyes and I think about the day. I think about how you answered my prayer and kept me out of trouble. I got a good mark at school and I had fun at the park. I even met up with my friends. But we had to run for cover cause the sky exploded with thunder and the clouds let out buckets of rain. God, I had a good day. Now, please calm me down and help me fall asleep. I need my strength for tomorrow.

PSALM 78

Bedtime stories, moral stories, funny tales, fairy tales, true stories, adventure stories... How many stories do I want? Well, how many stories are there? Stories from Dad and Mom, stories from long, long ago. Stories that teach me about God. Stories make me feel happy, they make me imagine lands far away. "Another one, please." I say. I will keep these stories and will share them with my own children one day. Stories have so much to say.

TELL ME A STORY

GOD'S POWER

God, you're famous for your support and guidance. Help me when I've acted badly. Forgive me for my mistakes. Don't leave me in this mess. I know you care, even when I've done something wrong. You still love me and you help me to start over. Thank you, God.

Smile Your Blessings on Me

God, you're like my strong shepherd. You lead your flock to a safe place. You take care of your sheep and you take care of your people, everywhere. You come near and smile your blessings on me. When I'm in trouble, you don't just hold my hand and lead the way; you pick me up in your arms and take me there. You save me and show me kindness.

PSALM 80

THANKS GIVING PARTY

It's a special day, a feast day! Come and celebrate with me! Listen! I hear songs from the choir, music from the band, noises from the trumpets and horns. It's like my birthday except it's in honor of you, God. It's not because it's your birthday but it's because of what you do. I guess it's like a huge thanksgiving day to remember all that you have done. Oh, my goodness! Oh, my yumminess! We're celebrating with cake and toppings, baked breads with honey and special spreads.

God, you stand up for the poor and the weak. You make sure that they don't get pushed and bullied around by bad people who don't care. You're the best judge there is because you do what's right and fair. Sometimes I yell for help because it seems the world is coming unglued and falling apart. Please nail it back in place. We need this world safe in your hands.

TOGETHER AGAIN

PSALM 82

BLOW IN THE WIND

God, don't forget about me. Please don't be silent.
The wind is ready to blow. Help, help! When scary
things happen around me, I think you're so far
away. I don't see you. God, please don't blow away
with the wind. Let the problems blow away instead.
It's cold. Please be a blanket around me. It's dark.
Be my shining light. I'm afraid. Be my strong
armor. Then everyone will know that you are
the most high God in all the earth.

PSALMS 83

HOW LOVELY IT IS

How lovely is your home, God. I dream about living there. I wonder if it's like a palace of joy, full of pretty songs. How blessed are those who live with you. They praise you always. There are cool springs and fresh pools of rain. One day spent with you is better than a 1000 days in the best vacation spot at the beach. You don't hold back anything from those who stay close to you.

Fruits of Blessings

God, you smiled on the earth. You gave me good times. You kept me from sin. Help me again. Don't give up on me. Show me your great big love. You promise peace for your people. Honesty sprouts green leaves from the ground. Respect pours down from the skies. God, you shine goodness and beauty everywhere you go. The land is filled with fruits of blessings. Help me to do what's right and be happy.

No one but you

God, please listen to me and answer. I'm trying to do the right thing here. Help your bunny. I depend on you from morning to night. I know I'm safe in your hands. You have a great big heart for all those who ask for help. Every time I'm in trouble I call on you and you come to the rescue. Let me parade your goodness and show off your beauty and the great things you do. Teach me to walk straight, on the right path. I love you, God, from head to toe.

PSALM 86

HOME SWEET HOME

God, a house is mainly walls and a roof, but a home is made up of everything inside it. A house might be big and strong and maybe decorated with the most beautiful furniture, but that doesn't make it a home. A home is a place where I feel safe. A place where I can relax and put my feet up as I read my favorite book, where I can play with my favorite toys and spend time with my most favorite people in the whole world. Home is a welcoming place. God, home is where you live. Thank you for my home, so cozy and safe.

PSALM 87

MY SAD CRY

God, you're my last chance. Please put
me on your calendar so that you're sure
to make time for me. Take some notes so
you know how to help me out. I've had a
bucketful of trouble. Now I need a handful
of help. I'm sending you this "HELP"
signal. It means "Save me!" I feel lost in a
maze and I can't find my way out.
Tears and frustration fill me to the brim.
Please help me out of this mess.

PSALM 88

LOVE GOES ON

Your love is my song, and I'll sing it all the day long. I tell my friends about it. How it goes on and on for always. Your love is the road I walk on. Your faithfulness is the roof over my head. Truth and fairness are the roots, my strong foundation. Love and honesty are the fruits. God, happy are those who know your password to enter into your presence. It's praise! I am thanking you in full. I'm telling others how good you are. I feel so happy. I feel I'm walking on air.

PSALM 89

BLESS IT

God, you have been around since the beginning. Even before the mountains were born, before the world was created, you were God. You are patient because you have all the time in the world. A thousand years or one day, it's all the same to you. We're like a blade of grass, that springs up with the sun but then it can be mowed down in a second. Life is here today but can be gone tomorrow. If there was a story written about me, some would be good and some probably not. I'm sorry for that. Please teach me to live well. Teach me to be wise and to be kind. And bless the work I do. Please make something beautiful out of it.

A PLACE OF SAFETY

I go to you, my God, to feel safe. You keep me from falls and tumbles. Your big stretched out arms protect me. I don't have to be afraid of the dark nor of the dangers during the day. Sickness and germs are all around me, but you keep me from them. I have made you my place of refuge, my home. I run to you to feel safe. No harm can get through the door because your angels are like my bodyguards. You give me the best of care. I trust you completely.

It's such a good thing to give thanks to you, God. I announce your love each morning and I sing about your care when night falls. I play for you on my music machine. Can you hear it? Each string makes a sound to you. It says "You make me happy". I smile, I laugh, I shout for joy. My ears hear of your love and faithfulness. Good people will prosper like palm trees and grow tall like pines, from living close to you. I want to be a strong and healthy tree, always bearing fruit. God, you are good and everything you do is good. You are my strength forever.

MY MUSIC MAKER

Hail to the King

PSALM 93

Hail to the king! God, you're the king and you're dressed with majesty. That means your clothes show beauty, power and strength. You stand mighty strong, unshakable and unmovable. Your throne and earth is set in place forever. Sea storms can be strong, real strong, with their loud roars, crashing waves and thunder bolts. But you are way more powerful than that. You rule high in the heavens and you rule down on earth. What you say always goes! My king, you rock! You rule!

God, you know everything. Even though some people try to get away with doing bad stuff, you see them. They're not smart at all to think they can fool you. But happy are those who learn from you. You teach me from your Word and you help my heart to do right. I have a quiet place to read and study, without distractions. Please help my little brain to learn this important stuff that I need to live a good life. The kind of stuff that pleases you.

LOTS TO LEARN

In His Hands

I will shout my praises to you, God. Let my joyful song raise the roof. You're a strong rock that is consistent, not easily moved or shaken. You're a refuge and strength. God, you made the earth and you've got the whole world in your hands. That means you have power and control over it all. The mountains and caves, the oceans and streams, they're all yours. You made me too and I'm all yours. Your great love cares for me like a shepherd cares for his sheep.

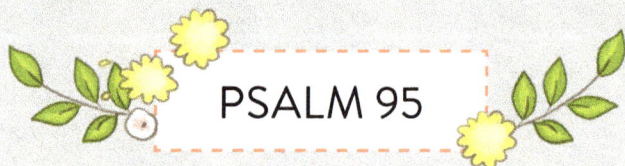

PSALM 95

MY GIFT TO GOD

Let me sing a new song! Earth and everyone, sing with me! I will shout the good news about you, God, from sea to sea. You are worth a thousand praises. Your power and beauty set you apart from fake gods. I bend down before you to bring you my special gift. Sky and earth, hills and seas, animals and trees, come join the band! We will all make music and dance a parade for you, our God. Here you come, to make all things right. Bravo to you!

PSALM 96

BEAUTIFUL

God, you rule! That's something to shout about. My shout is a happy shout, to show how excited I am. It says "Let's party! Let's celebrate!" God, I look at your creation. It's beautiful. From the smallest to the biggest, from the shortest to the tallest; these pretty flowers smell so good. And imagine that they come from a tiny little seed in the ground. I began as a little seed too. You also plant seeds of joy in my heart and it makes me glow and bounce in cheer. I shout "thank you" for your goodness.

PSALM 97

LET'S PARTY!

A world of wonders made by a God of wonders! That's you, God. You rolled up your sleeves and got to work to set things in place. So many stories tell of what you've done, but I even get to see some with my own eyes. I can't even count them on my fingers and toes, there are too many. A huge big bonus is that you love me. Everything you do is a reason for a celebration. So we're setting up a barbecue and inviting our friends for a party. I've even invited my pet goldfish. He'll blow bubbles to show his thanks. My friends and I like to bounce the ball and dance around and sing to show our thanks. I can't wait for the relay races and games. Oh, and best of all, the dessert. I feel so blessed, God. Thank you.

PSALM 98

God, you rule over everything. You tower way higher than all the rulers of the world, and over all the big famous names. If it was a beauty contest you would win it. God, you're the best! You are strong and you make things right when they're crooked or off balance. You punish the wrong but you forgive those who are sorry. I make mistakes and "oopsies" too. Your great big love washes them clean and helps me start over again. Thank you.

YOU FORGIVE

I'M FULL OF JOY

I bounce for joy, I shout and cheer, for you are here! God, I come before you with singing and laughing. Whether I do a dance or take a swing, whether I take a nap or eat something, I do it happily. I know that you are God and that you made me. I belong to you. I enter a special place with the password "Thank you". It works every time. A circle of praise makes me feel right at home with you. God, you are all goodness and all love, for always and forever.

PSALM 100

I took a walk to the garden this morning. I whistled and sang as I journeyed along. Then I found this branch. *This would make a great gift for Dad and Mom,* I thought. And so I began to decorate it. First with a necklace of pretty flowers, then I blew kisses of love all over it. And now to take it home... it seems like such a long way away. Dear God, please give me strength. I'm trying my best here with this very heavy branch. But I won't give up. I want my parents to be proud of me and pleased with my gift.

MY BEST

Sick of being sick

God, please listen to my crying and hear my prayer for help. Pay attention to me and come quickly. I'm feeling miserable. I have a fever and a headache. My body is really sick. I can't eat much and my legs are weak from laying in bed so long. I'm so sick of being sick. When will this be over? I'm like a lonely bird on a roof. Please don't forget about me. I want to get better. I want to jump around and play with my friends again. I want to sing and dance and remember all the good things you have done for me. Give me back full strength. I know you can do it. I want to be as good as new. Things get old and die but you are always the same. Please help me, God.

PSALM 102

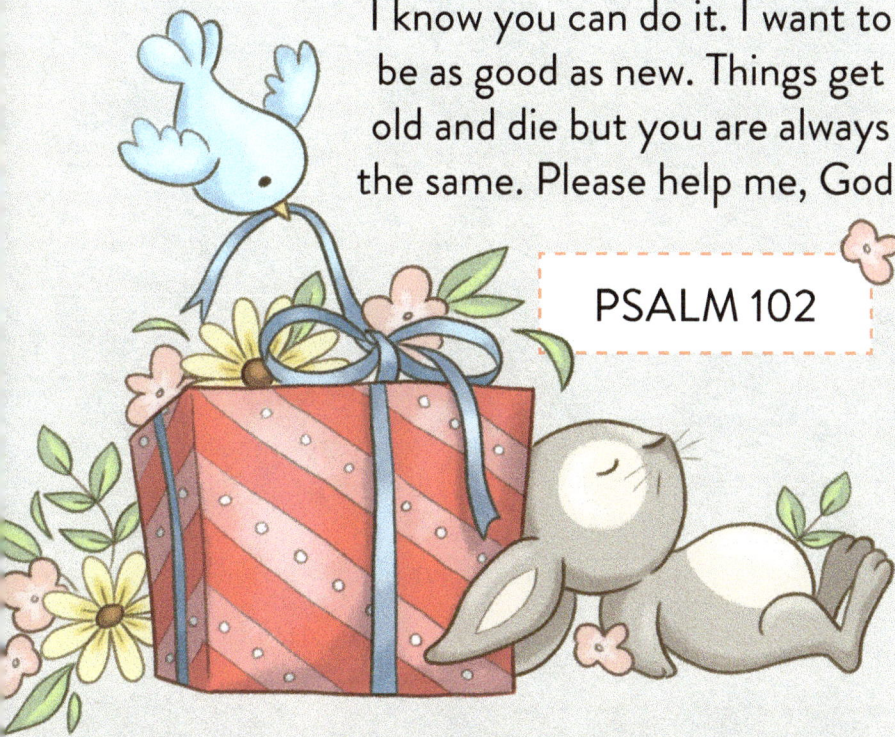

With all of me I praise you, God. From my head to my toes, I bless your name. I won't forget your kindness to me. You forgive my wrongs and you heal my ouchies. You pile up bunches of love and mercy and you wrap me in a bouquet of goodness. You make everything come out all right. Even bad times or disappointments can turn out okay. You do what's right and fair. As high as the sky is above the earth, that's how great your love is for those who respect you. From the east to the west, that's how wide you show mercy. Flowers don't last forever. They wilt and die. But your love is the only thing that goes on and on and on and on and on and...

ALL GOOD

PSALM 103

RICH WITH GOODNESS

PSALM 104

Oh, God, how great you are! You are dressed up in sunshine and your glory spreads out over the whole sky. You said it, and it happened. The earth was formed. You give us everything on this earth and it makes us happy. Everything is timed in perfect order, God. The day and the night, the animals and the seasons, the plants and the trees. The earth is rich with your goodness.

I jump and I shout "Hallelujah!" That's how I show my thanks, God! I tell others what you have done. I translate my praises into musical tunes. I keep my eyes open to see your wonders and notice your presence. 'Cause with you, everything goes way better. You keep your promises, all the way from my great-great-great-grandparents until forever. You were with Abraham, Jacob, Joseph and Moses, and their stories are a reminder that you will care for me too.

For Keeps

PSALM 105

THE JOY OF FRIENDS

God, I feel good when I do the right thing. I'm one happy bunny when I learn a new good habit, without being reminded about it. That kind of shows I'm growing up, right?

God, thank you for the joy of having friends. Your love is forever. You're invited to our play time, anytime you like. We have so much fun, especially when you're a part of it, God. But, oops! There were times when my friend and I didn't get along and we squabbled. We each wanted our own way. Please help us learn from our past mistakes so that we can enjoy all our times together.

As deep as....

You're an oceanful of love, God. That's a lot of love, enough to go around and around for a long time. When I don't know what to do, or when I feel lost with no help in sight, you come to the rescue. You steer my wheel in the right direction. You pull me out of trouble and keep me from getting all wet. I love being out at sea. That's when I see you in action. With one word, you send the wind over here. With one point, you send the waves over there. As wide as the ocean and as deep as the sea, is your great love for me.

PSALM 107

WE LIFT YOU HIGH

I'm ready, God, ready from head to toe. I'm ready to sing and raise my voice up high. Wake up everyone! Come on! The music bubbles up in our hearts and we feel the beat. Let's sing our joy, dance the wonder and chant in style. We'll raise the roof with our praise. Let's join all of outer space, as we shout out our thanks. God, up, up, up, we lift you high. Up, up, up, you lift us out of trouble. You burst with joy as you tell us how much you love us. You will never leave us. With your help, we are strong.

PSALM 108

PSALM 109

Love scores!

God, do not be silent as I pray and ask for help. Some people tell lies about me. They call me names and hurt me for no good reason. But why? I try my best to be kind and not get angry in return, 'cause that would only make things worse. But I need a little help here 'cause I feel my love is emptying out quickly. God, your love is big enough for all of us. Please give me some of yours so people can see and know of your love too. They can do all the bad they want, but nothing can keep them away from your love. Your love scores highest!

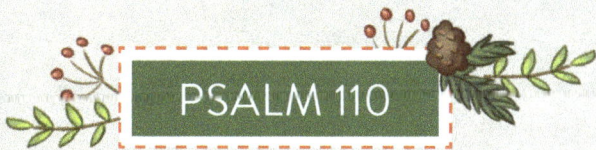

I sit by your side, God, until you have done your work and taken control over the situation. At times things turn out better when I just do nothing at all. I will stay patiently until you tell me it's time to do something. This is the best place of all. Side by side with you, is my favorite place to be. I'm at peace as you show your strength and smooth things out.

Side by Side

GOD CRAFTS

With all of my imagination, I thank you God. You bring me joy that never stops. You add a special touch to life that makes it amazing. God, only you can do that. Your goodness is made to last. Your kindness never gets old or out of date. It's rust and water proof. Wisdom comes from respecting you, God. And your style fits me perfectly. It's like you know my favorite color, shape, texture and size that suits me best. You understand me, and I praise you forever.

PSALM 112

God, I try my best to do what's right. We even have family goals in my house. Here they are: "Show respect. Always tell the truth. Be kind. Do your best. Be happy. Don't give up. Say please and thank you. Try new things. Apologize. Forgive. Dream big. Have fun!" To be honest, when I follow these goals, I feel really happy. And when I do the right thing at the right time, I get the most out of every occasion.

FAMILY GOALS

THANK YOU

I love you, God and I love to praise you. But sometimes I don't know what to say, so I just say over and over, "Thank you...thank you..." I think you know what my heart means when I do that. My love for you fills up those empty spaces. Every time I think of you, I thank you. When I wake up, I thank you for the day. When I get dressed, I thank you for my clothes. I thank you for water to brush my teeth, for food to fill up my snack box. A couch and a pillow to sit all cozy, and a family that loves me... There are loads more. I could go on and on and on.

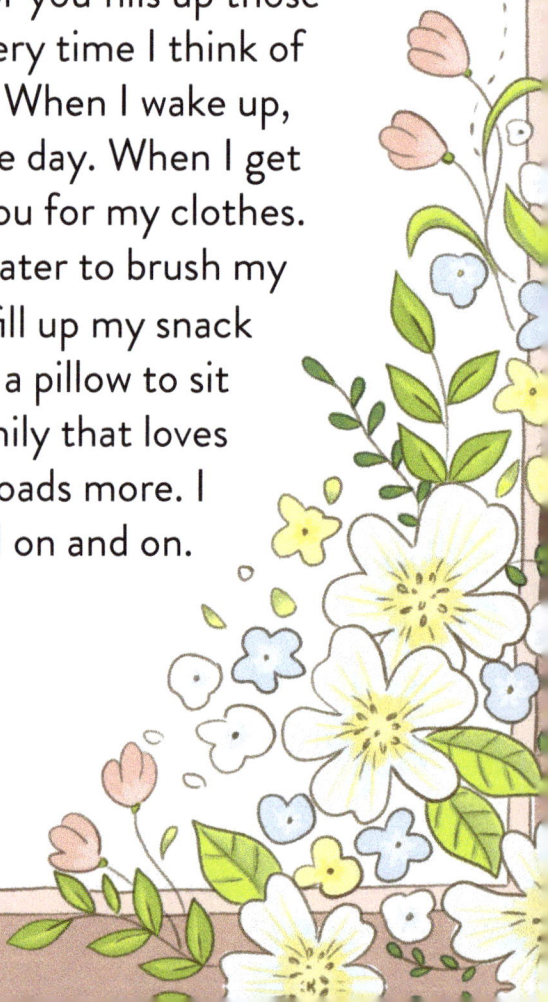

HE DID IT ALL

God, you have BIG power. In times passed, you divided the Red Sea, you made the Jordan River turn back. You made the mountains and the hills dance around. And you can still use your BIG power today. Whatever you say, it happens. You could shake a mountain and make it move to another place. You could turn a rock into a pool of water or a dry ground into a stream. If you can do all those big things, I know that you can certainly do little things for little me.

YOU REMEMBER

All praise belongs to you, God. No one needs to wonder where you are, because you show yourself in the heavens and in everything beautiful. You are here and everywhere. Each flower reminds me of your love. Each leaf reminds me of your faithfulness. You're not a fake god made of brick or metal. You're not fake that you can't speak or see, hear or smell. I choose you, God! I respect you and I put my trust in you because you keep me safe. You remember me and you bless my whole family, from the biggest to the smallest, from the oldest to the youngest. Thank you for helping my family grow rich in happiness.

PSALM 115

PSALM 116

AT YOUR SERVICE

Thank you, God, for listening to my plea for help. I got stuck in a puddle and then my tire went Poof! I didn't know what to do. But problems are an occasion for you to come and do something. You sent Dad my way to help fix my tire. Then you sent the rain to wash off the mud. Now I can go on my merry way! Oops, but I'd better look straight ahead, so that I don't land in that thorny bush. God, how can I say thanks? Oh, I know! I'll sit here a bit to relax and share my snack with you. I say "Cheers to God!" as I raise my cup of juice. I'm here for you, God. At your service!

A SONG OF PRAISE

Praise God, everybody! Applaud for him, all people, all creatures, all animals big or small! The birds sing their song. People say it in words or sounds. Bunnies do their bounce. Flowers show their pretty colors. We praise you, God, each in the way we know best. We thank you because you fill up our lives with love, each day. You are the most wonderful thing in the whole wide world. I love you.

PSALM 117

NOW TO TODAY!

Thank you, God. You are all good and your love never quits, never gives up, never ends. It's not like a battery powered toy car that only lasts a short while. It goes on for always and always. Even further than a real car that has to stop for gas or engine repairs. I'm so glad it worked out to go camping with Dad. This is so exciting! God, this is the best day of my life. I'm sitting in my seat, but I'm jumping for joy on the inside. You have given today an extra special touch of goodness and I've got an extra boost of gladness to share.

PSALM 119

God, I feel happy when I stay on course and follow your directions. How can I live a good life? By carefully reading the map of your Word. Your Word is like a lamp to my feet and a light for my path. Your Word comforts me in my troubles and helps me find solutions to my problems. I delight in your Word, God. It is sweet to my soul, even sweeter than cake and ice-cream. I read your Word and my heart says WOW! It is full of wisdom and smartness. Keep my eyes open to your Word, God. I feel so relaxed and at peace when I read it. It gives me new strength for the day.

GOD'S WORD

PEACE PLEASE

Hey neighbors, let's be friends. Let's not fight. Why lie and cheat behind each other's backs? That's no fun. Instead, why don't we help each other out? If you need help to water your garden, I'll be there as quick as a flash. And when I need help to pick apples, maybe you could help me out. We can get so much more done by working together. Wanna come to a party? Let's have a peace party and put up this peace banner. It means no more fighting, no more lies, no more complaining. I want peace. I want happy neighbors. And most of all, I hope I can be a good neighbor and a good friend to you.

PSALM 120

Shade from the Sun

I look up to you, God. That's where I go to find help because strength comes from you. You made all of heaven and earth and you keep me safe. You don't even take a break or stop for a nap. You are always guarding, always protecting. You're like my umbrella shielding me from the hot sun during the day. And you're my warm blanket at night. I turn on my little night light and it reminds me that you are close by. You keep me safe while I'm out and you comfort me when I get home. You guard me now, and you always will.

PSALM 121

Dad and Mom called, "Let's go to the house of God!" My heart jumped for joy. And now we're here, we're here! It's a beautiful place, a big place. It's bright and cheery. It's a house of praise after all. But God, I can praise you anytime and anywhere, right? I don't have to be in a certain house or building to praise you. But, having a special place just for worship reminds me that it's important. I have a little tent in the garden. Could that work as my house of praise? I like to go to my quiet, cozy spot to think about you and praise you. You are good to me, God. All I want to do is thank you.

PSALM 122

A PLACE TO PRAISE

LEAN ON YOU

I look to you, God. Like a student looks up to their teacher or a child looks up to their papa and mama, I look up to you. I lean on you because you are rock strong. Ouchy! My feet are sore from so much walking on my own. Sometimes I'm clumsy and I fall and I trip. You bend down and put on a band aid. Then when my little legs can't take another step, you pick me up for a piggy-back ride. Up here with you, they already feel better. I'm so glad I can lean on you, God. We all need somebody to lean on.

 PSALM 123

What If?

PSALM 124

God, if it hadn't been for you, I would be... Oh, my! I think I'd still be stuck in that pond, all wet and drippy. Or maybe I would have been bitten by that dragonfly. That little fishy would have pocked at me too. And I would probably have fallen off that rock. Imagine that? But you didn't take off and leave me alone. God, thank you, thank you. You, who made heaven and earth, and all these little creatures. Please continue to stay close by, for always. Help me to do the right thing and to keep away from harm.

Those who put their trust in you, God, are safe like a mountain. Not just any mountain, a metal-strong mountain. Nothing can move it, nothing can shake it. Mountains often surround towns and cities. God, you surround your people. You draw circles of protection around me and nothing can get in. Bad people, mean people, bully people, try to break through. But your magic bubble of love is bullet-proof, made of the strongest material ever. I do my best to obey and do the right thing and then I trust you for the rest. With you comes perfect peace.

PSALM 125

YOU CIRCLE AROUND ME

FULL OF JOY

Do I remember feeling really happy? A time of celebration? That was you God, at work! I partied, I laughed, I sang, I bounced with joy. You did great things for me and it made me glad. Do I remember feeling sad? Crying and tears running down my face? Yes. But God, you were there as well. Lots of work and pain goes into planting, preparing the ground, weeding, pruning and then harvesting. But then comes celebration and enjoying the fruit of my hard work. God, you have done great things for me and my heart is filled with joy. Mmmm. And now my tummy is also full of goodness.

PSALM 126

MY FAMILY

PSALM 127

God, you're the master builder. You build our homes and families. You draw up the plans and you provide the tools and all the material. Then you work right beside us. No need for us to get stressed, to work too hard or get too tired. We build together with you, God, and then we can rest in peace. Children are precious gifts from you, God. And little babies are the cutest of all. I can't wait to get home from school and hold my little baby brother. I'm a proud big brother times three. Together, we make up one very happy family, safe and sound in our happy home.

Happy are those who show respect and who obey. That's our family motto and because of it, we enjoy so many joyful moments together. Papa sits at the head of the table with a great big smile. Mama brings out our favorite meal with a grin and a twinkle in her eye. A happy papa and mama make happy kids. Yay for family dinner time! Yes, yes, for family play time! We all like to hear those yeses. God, you also say yes and our home overflows with your goodness and blessings.

HAPPY TIMES

WON'T GIVE UP

Those pesky weeds choke up my plants. No good at all. Out you go! Out with all your fellow mates of thorns and thistles, rocks and pebbles. You don't belong in my garden. Just like mean bullies don't belong here either. They try to choke out my joy when they kick and poke and make fun. Out with the pesky bullies! But I'm not giving up on you, little plants. Whew! It's tiring, but I gotta work hard to make you grow beautifully. And I want those flowers and carrot plants to grow and smile real big. Do you think there's hope for bullies as well? I bet if I water them with lots of kindness, they could smile real big too.

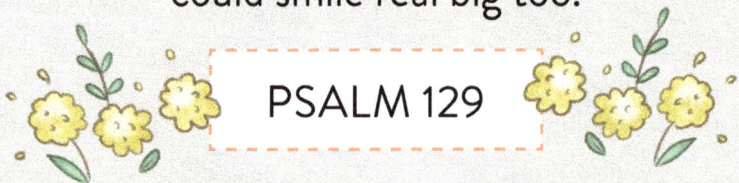

PSALM 129

God, I was just thinking... do you keep notes of all my mistakes? Do you remember all those naughty things I did when I was little, or now that I'm bigger? I hope not. If you did, I wouldn't stand a chance. As it turns out, you forgive. Forgiveness is what you do best. That means you erase any trace of those bad notes and bad marks. Thank you, God. You give me another chance to get it right. This time I pray and ask for your help. And I wait for you here.

I wait a little longer, until you show me what to do. And when you're ready, you just fill me to the brim with love and forgiveness.

I WAIT

Shhhh, my heart. Rest now and get quiet. I close my eyes and I rest in you, God. Thoughts, stop rushing. Body, stop jittering. Relax. I breathe in and out slowly and get still. Big ideas can wait, worries and fears can drift away. For right now I'm in your loving arms, God, just like a little baby in his mama's arms. He feels love, comfort, and is content. Help me to trust like that little baby. Let me be content for this very moment, and feel in perfect peace.

BABY TRUST

"We're having guests over tonight!" Mama says. "They can use my bed," I tell her. Yes, yes, I'll set it up just right for them. You'll see, it will be perfect. It's okay if I sleep somewhere else for tonight. And if I don't sleep so comfortably, well, it's only one night. Guests must have the best! My bed is soft and warm. "Oh, Mama, can I help make the special dinner too?" Then I set the table with our best dishes and serve our favorite juice. I put on my nice clothes to look my best. Mama says I look sharp. I hope they feel welcome and I hope this makes them smile. Dear God, you can visit our home too, you know. Any time!

THE VERY BEST

In it together

It's good, it's great, it's wonderful when friends are friends and family is family. It's good, it's great, it's wonderful when brothers and sisters get along well. Living in unity, feeling like we belong, enjoying each other and sharing, this is God's precious gift. Like sweet rain after a hot day, like joy bubbling up, like coming home. God, you meant life to be lived together, and you bless us with love and unity, now and forever.

PSALM 134

God, I look up at the sunset sky. WOW! It's beautiful! I get quiet and think about your goodness. I tell you that I love you... Oops, but I'd better get going with my bed-prep now. There's work to be done. God, please come join me; that way my work can also be a praise to you. Ok, I've got to clear the table, brush my teeth, take a bath, fold my clothes... I lift up my hands and give my clothes a twirl. I hum as I brush my teeth, which makes tons of bubbles so I feel extra clean. Doing this together with you God, is making my bedtime routine sparkle with fun.

WITH YOU

OCEANS AND SKIES

Hallelujah! That's a big word to say "I praise you, God!" I praise you for your goodness and love. Sometimes I do it at church, but I don't have to wait for then. I can praise you right here and now, whenever I feel like it. It's easy for me to think of you here; I just look at the beautiful sky and the mighty ocean. Yes! I confirm your greatness, God. You do as you please and it's pleasing to me too. My favorite is making sandcastles and splashing in the waves, while exploring all your amazing little creations. I hold Dad's hand when a pinching creature comes along. It puts me at ease and it reminds me that you're right here. Thank you, God.

I give thanks to you, God, for you are good. I sing about the great things you have done. Your faithful kindness lasts forever! I could repeat that a billion times over and over again, but that still wouldn't be enough to count your love. If I had a sand timer, it would never run out, that's how much love you have! I feel your kindness through my loving family. I see your kindness in your beautiful and special creations. I remember your kindness when I feel sad and you make me happy again.

FOR ALWAYS

PSALM 136

DON'T FORGET

PSALM 137

When I want to remember something important, I write it down, or I jot myself a note. That way, it's for keeps. But I can't forget what you do, God. It's too amazing, too grand to forget. It would be like forgetting to eat my breakfast or to play with my toys. I don't do that. It's on my mind and I do it everyday. Sometimes I make up songs for my times tables or spelling words at school. I remember the songs and then I remember the words and numbers. That's kind of cool. But singing for you and about you is only pleasure. You're always on my mind because you are everywhere.

Thank you, God. Everything in me says "Thank you!" Your love is solid and it doesn't give up on me. You shout "Go! Go! Go!" and it sparks courage. Your name gives strength! Sometimes I have a bad day and it leads to a bad play. I call out "Coach!" and you come swiftly. You give me tips and tricks to help me do better. When I stumble and fall you lift me up. Your pat on the back gives me strength to run faster and to kick harder. Thank you, Coach, for your promise to look out for me. You have big plans for me. Help me finish what we started. I don't want to quit now. I want to make it to the finals.

COURAGE, CHILD!

PSALM 138

God, you know all about me. I'm never out of your sight. You even know what I'm going to say before I say it. I look behind me and you're there. Then up ahead and you're there too. Just to know that you're always here with me, is too wonderful to understand. Though I couldn't play "Hide and seek" with you very well, 'cause there is no place you couldn't find me. Even a dark place is not dark to you. You made me and formed me in Mama's tummy. Body and all, I am amazingly made. You know everything about me. So much care!

YOU KNOW ME

PSALM 139

A BAD TRAP

God, please save me from troublemakers. They think up new ways to be bad and they start fights wherever they go. They make traps to get me, they plot ways to trip me up and then they make fun of me. Please, God, keep me far from them. I know you listen to my prayer. Don't let them have their way. You're on the side of those who do the right thing and you care when someone gets hurt. I don't feel worried one bit 'cause I feel safe with you.

God, hello! Hello! It's me! Can you hear me? Can you smell the cologne I put on? I'm calling to say goodnight! Oh, yes! I had a great day! Play time was a blast! But is there a way you could put a guard over my mouth? What I mean is that sometimes I get in trouble for saying the wrong things. I want to keep my mouth closed when I feel like spouting off bad words. Yes, God, I know that the very best is to use kind and honest words. What's that? Oh, yes, I'm going to bed now. Yes, thank you, God. I know you're right here beside me. Actually I don't really have to call you on this thing, but it's fun. I feel all grown up when I use the phone. Thank you, God for keeping me safe. Goodnight! See you in the morning!

PSALM 141

About Today

WHICH WAY?

I'm lost! Help! Help! I don't know which way. Papa and Mama were just here. Where did they go? Oops, I guess it was me who went the wrong way. I'm sorry, God. There are so many doors and secret rooms in this old place, and they all look the same. How am I going to find my way? Where is the exit? Oh, I should have stayed close. But God, you can hear me now, even in this old place. Please, help me to be found as I wait here. I won't stray again, no I won't. I really want to continue this exciting old castle adventure, together with my family. It's always best that way!

PSALM 143

I could really use a refreshing drink right now and it looks like these flowers could use one too. I get thirsty for you, God. When I feel empty and my energy is drained, your answers come like the perfect drink. I love to wake up each day and hear your "Good morning!" call. And as I go to sleep at night, I'm in perfect peace, knowing that you're still right here. Please teach me how to live. I point my eyes, my ears and my heart to you, ready to listen. You refresh and make new.

NEED A DRINK?

JUST A LITTLE SEED

All praise to you, God. You're like my home, my very favorite place to be. Home is where I feel safe and loved. But God, what am I to you? I feel so small, like a tiny seed, or a puff of air. Do I really matter to you? You come and pay attention to me. Imagine that! First you make sure I'm okay, and if not, you help me out of trouble. Then you cover me with your love, from head to toe. You must also care for your little plants. They seem happy and grow beautifully. Make me tall and strong too, bearing fruit of goodness. Now I sing with joy 'cause I feel happy and blessed.

PSALM 145

WITH LOVE

I give praise to you, God. With all my love, I send you thanks. Let me be grateful every day, for everything that comes my way. Your greatness reaches to the highest peak. It's so high I can't get over it. It's so wide I can't get around it. Oh, wonderful love! You feed, you clothe, you help the weak. Your beauty makes the news, your wonders go viral! I could write a book, I could sing a song, I could make a movie, but nothing would be able to express all your goodness. You are rich in love, with pocketfuls of mercy. You are patient and kind and slow to become angry. With all my love, I say thank you, God.

HE FEEDS

Thank you, God! You don't just take care of me, you take GREAT care of me. You go higher, deeper and wider than I could ask for. You're in charge and I put my hope in you. I don't have to worry one bit. You give bountiful blessings. I am overwhelmed with today's treasures. You provide all my needs and I'm completely content.

I love to praise and thank you, God. Saying *thank you* is a beautiful thing. It's fitting to any season or any occasion. I'm amazed how you pay attention to every detail. Spring comes once a year, and the birds sing their song for all to hear. Summer will soon arrive! The sun, the flowers and the plants come alive. Autumn brings wind and changing of leaves. Beautiful colors fall from the trees. Winter blows cold all around, snow piles up on the frozen ground. But little creatures are fed all throughout the year, they're in your good care, there's no need to fear.

PSALM 147

CHANGING SEASONS

ALL CREATURES

PSALM 148

I can praise you, God, from a high mountain, or from under the sea. From up on my bunk bed, to down in my basement. Every creature you have made praises you. From cute and cuddly pets to big ferocious-teeth-and-clawed animals. Furry animals, scaly animals, giant animals and teensy animals. It doesn't matter what size or shape or color or texture. As for us, it doesn't matter what age, what height or what culture. We can ALL praise you, our amazing, wonderful, spectacular God. You welcome us all!

PSALM 149

If I were a bird, I would use my wings. If I were a centipede, I would use all my legs. If I were a singer I would use my voice. If I were an artist, I would use my hands. Because I'm your child, I will use everything, all of me, to share your glory. Dancing uses every bit of me. I get in the mood of the music and I swing my arms to the sky. I bounce my legs and kick them high. I follow the beat as I tap my feet. God, it brings me great joy to give you praise.

THE PRAISE DANCE

THE PRAISE BAND

I praise you God, in your holy place, I praise you God, for your grace. I praise you because you are strong. Your goodness goes on and on. I blow a trumpet, loud and sharp. I strum a guitar and pluck a harp. Tambourines, help keep the beat. Dancers, get on your feet. Lips on flutes, hands on a violin; play them well, make them sing. Cymbals, or any other instrument you like. Join the band, give a hand. Let everything that takes in air, share God's praises everywhere.

THE END

TO PONDER

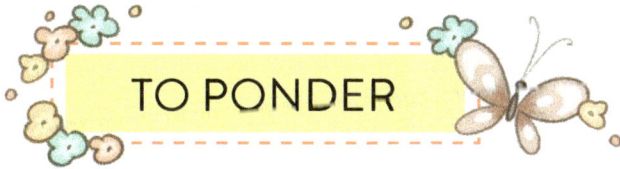

What is my favorite Psalm?

What makes it special to me?

If I could write a Psalm, what would it be about?

How would I start it?

What Psalm best fits my day today?

What Psalm would I give to encourage a friend?

How do these Psalms make me feel?

ABOUT THE AUTHOR

Agnes de Bezenac is a children's author/illustrator and has over 150 published books. Her passion is to help contribute a little extra joy and meaning through her creations.

Agnes is a mom of two and lives together with her husband in a little French town. Her past times are drawing, decorating, organizing and using her creativity to help brighten people's day.

From Agnes: "The book of Psalms has often brought me comfort and joy. It's a reminder that though life is tough, we don't have to go at it alone. Times of trouble and grief are eased when meditating on God's faithfulness. It's wonderful to be able to bring our feelings and emotions to a higher power through prayer, a song or a psalm. I felt that if these Psalms can speak to us big folks, there is surely something for the little ones too. Thus came about this project of child-friendly Psalms. My hope is that children will be touched and comforted and that this book can help make their day a little brighter."

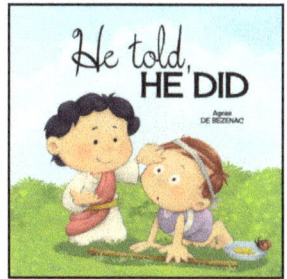

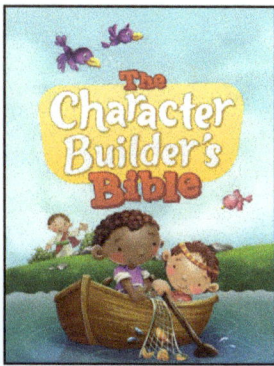

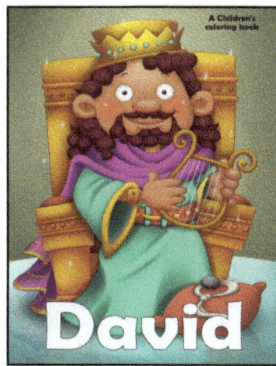

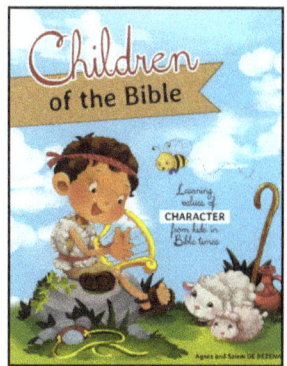

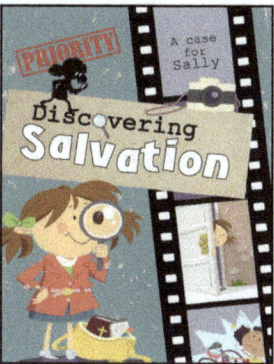

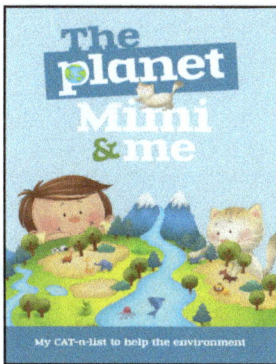

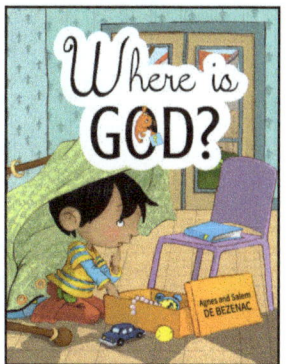

Wise words
Taken from the Book of Proverbs in the Bible

The Armor of God
Ephesians 6:10-18
Agnes DE BEZENAC

He told, HE DID
Agnes DE BEZENAC

The Character Builder's Bible

David
A Children's coloring book

Children of the Bible
Learning values of CHARACTER from kids in Bible times
Agnes and Salem DE BEZENAC

Discovering Salvation
PRIORITY
A case for Sally

The planet Mimi & me
My CAT-n-list to help the environment

Where is GOD?
Agnes and Salem DE BEZENAC

MORE BOOKS

iCHARACTER

Visit our website www.iCharacter.org for
more kids books and downloads.

Published by iCharacter Limited ®. (Ireland)
Written by Agnes de Bezenac
Illustrated by Agnes de Bezenac
Colored by Adina and Agnes de Bezenac
Copyright 2020. All rights reserved.
www.iCharacter.org